Farm Life

Copyright © 2021 by

NEVADA THORNTON

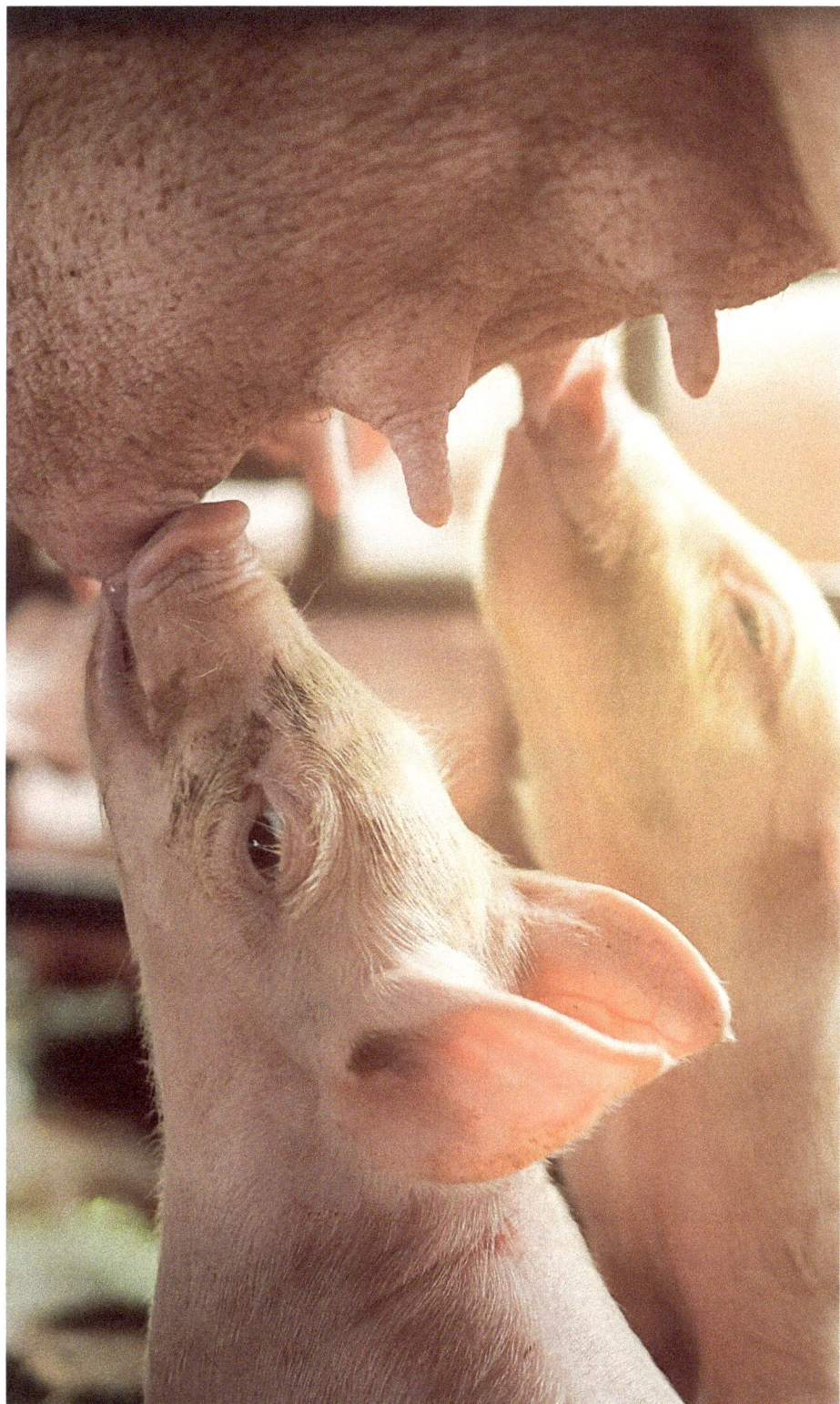

More picture books by Nevada Thornton

1.Beautiful Flowers
2.Adorable Babies
3.Pet Laughs
4.Cooking And Recipes
5.Farm Life
6.Beautiful Butterflies
7.Beautiful Birds
8.Beach Holiday

Beautiful Butterflies

NEVADA THORNTON

Beautiful Birds

NEVADA THORNTON

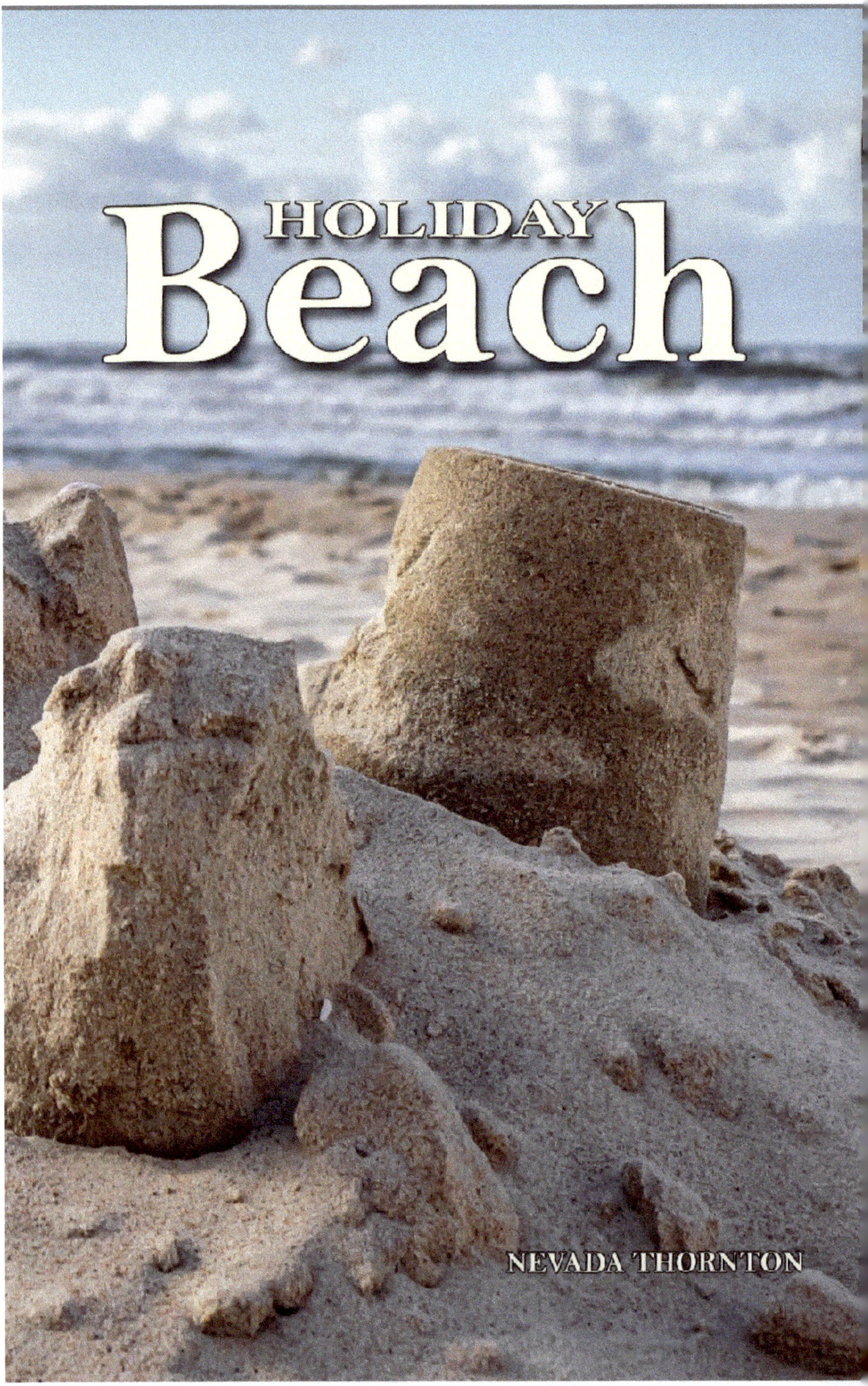
HOLIDAY
Beach
NEVADA THORNTON

Food and Cooking

NEVADA THORNTON

www.ingramcontent.com/pod-product-compliance
Lightning Source LLC
Chambersburg PA
CBHW040910210326
41597CB00029B/5033